WineStyle
MONTEREY COUNTY

BAY PUBLISHING COMPANY
Monterey, California

ISBN 0-9742147-0-1

Published by Bay Publishing Company
395 Del Monte Center, #103
Monterey, California 93940
www.baypublishing.com

Design by Andrea Gregg

Library of Congress
Cataloging-in-Publication
Data available.

CONTRIBUTORS

Contributors

We would like to thank all of the wineries and businesses that helped make this book come to life.

A Taste of Monterey

Anapamu Vineyards

Arroyo Seco Vineyards

Blackstone Winery

Chalone Vineyard

Château Julien Wine Estate

Cypress Inn

Fandango Restaurant

Hames Valley Vineyards

J. Lohr Vineyards and Winery

Jekel Vineyards

Mer Soleil Vineyard

Monterey County Vintners & Growers Association

Nielsen Brothers Market

Passionfish Restaurant

Sardine Factory Restaurant

Ventana Vineyards/Meador Estate

CONTENTS

WineStyle
MONTEREY COUNTY

MONTEREY COUNTY VINTNERS & GROWERS ASSOCIATION

A World Class Wine Producing Region . . .

. . . Monterey County is ripe with nature's bounty: beautiful, rugged coastlines, soaring mountains, clean air, verdant valleys blessed with a climate that features abundant sunshine and the gentle cooling kiss of evening fog from the Pacific Ocean. Add to that mix ancient, alluvial soils that are perfect for growing wine grapes and the result is a world-class wine producing region.

The central coast region has always attracted people with an artistic, yet entrepreneurial bent—perfect qualities for the wine business. Some are native sons and daughters, others transplants, but all share a common love and passion for the art and science of wine making. Each approach the process from different angles and at differing paces, but all achieve the same outcome: the finest wines it is possible to produce at a given location. And every one of those wines is indelibly stamped with the personality and character of those that brought them to life.

Those wines have won countless awards and accolades in competition with those from the greatest, centuries-old wine producing regions of France, Italy and other areas. They have been served at Presidential inaugurations and have graced the tables of kings, queens and other world leaders. Wine from Monterey County can be found on the wine lists of the finest restaurants in the world and are recommended by top chefs and sommeliers everywhere.

But how did this all happen? What is it that catches the notoriously fickle attention and adoration of wine lovers?

The typical consumer does not think of wine as an agricultural product. Wine has a cachet, a mystique, an almost mythical quality that conjures up visions of elegant dinners and romantic interludes—not drip irrigation and heavy farm equipment. But agricultural it is, and serious business too. In 2001, wine grape production in Monterey County topped 180,000 tons valued at well over $200,000,000. More than fifty vineyards cultivate 45,000 acres planted in 21 different grape varieties of *Vinis Vinifera*, the species of grapes used to make wine.

The number one industry in Monterey County is agriculture. For decades, the Salinas Valley has been known as the "Salad Bowl of the World"—deservedly so, for also in 2001, growers there produced more than $650 *million* worth of lettuce of all varieties. Toss that with hundreds of thousands of tons of celery, tomatoes, onions, carrots, peppers and artichokes, and you've got a very large salad indeed.

It was in the 1960s that U.C. Davis Professor A.J. Winkler published a report that categorized California grape growing areas according to climate. Monterey County was classified as Type I, II and III regions on a scale of V, with I being the coolest. This placed the county on a par climatologically with the Napa Valley, and soon, some of the biggest names in the Napa wine business were planting vines in the Salinas Valley. But wine had been produced in the county long before Professor Winkler performed his study.

The story began more than two centuries ago, when wine grapes were planted by Franciscan friars at *La Mission San Antonio de Padua*, established by Father Junipero Serra in 1771 west of present-day King City. Wine was important to those Spanish friars for many reasons, not the least of which was its essential role in the celebration of the Roman Catholic Mass. Being European, the padres also viewed wine as an indispensable part of meals. Given the distances involved and the modes of transportation available, they deduced that if a steady supply were to be assured, the friars would have to take matters into their own hands. The vines they planted were known as "Mission Grapes," and they migrated with the friars from Loreto in Baja California in the south to Mission Sonoma in the north. The exact provenance of this variety is not known, but some believe it to be a hybrid of a Spanish *Vinifera* and a species of wild California grapes. Some of the vines planted by Serra's padres still survive at Mission San Antonio. The oldest commercially producing vines in the county were planted in 1919, and are in the Chalone AVA.

In the United States, wine growing regions are designated as American Viticultural Areas, or AVAs. These designations, also called appellations, were created by the government as a way for wine-makers to establish a geographical pedigree for their products. At last count, there were 137 AVAs in the U.S., and 12 more under review. In Monterey County there are seven, of which the Monterey AVA is by far the largest. The other six, *Carmel Valley, Santa Lucia Highlands, Arroyo Seco, Chalone, San Lucas and Hames Valley* either overlap or are adjoined to the Monterey AVA. Each is unique, however, in soil, climate and growing conditions. As a result of this diversity, many different wine grape varietals thrive in the area.

But what really sets the Monterey County region apart is the climate. For many of the AVAs in Monterey County, the combination of warm days and cool, foggy nights provides for an exceptionally long growing season. The vines tend to bud about two weeks sooner, and the fall

harvest typically takes place two weeks later than other regions, giving the fruit an extra bit of "hang time." That translates into smaller grapes with very concentrated fruit flavors. The extra month also lets the fruit mature more slowly, resulting in intense flavors and a nice balance of sugar and acidity. The southern Monterey County AVAs are much warmer than the majority of those in the north, yet the moderate influx of cool air from the Monterey Bay still makes its presence felt.

Monterey County is also famous for hospitality, and has been since the early days of recorded history. For well more than a

century, some of the finest and most famous hotels, resorts and restaurants in the world have been located in the county. Following in this rich tradition, there are 20 wine tasting rooms throughout the county where visitors can sample the various fruits of the vine produced here. Many have picnic areas where visitors can dine alfresco while enjoying stunning views of the valley below. In some cases, the winemakers themselves are on hand, eager to share their passion and love for the art of winemaking. In the Salinas Valley, signposts have been erected along the back roads to direct visitors to the wineries and tasting rooms.

As if wine lovers needed another reason to visit Monterey County, there are several wine themed events held in various venues throughout the area. In November, The Great Wine Escape Weekend features winery open houses, bus and self-guided tours of vineyards and wineries, concerts, and a Grand Finale tasting event. A favorite of many are the winemaker dinners, held at various restaurants and wineries that feature food and wine pairings custom tailored for the event. In many cases, collaborations between winemaker and chef produce memorable and unique food and wine pairings.

In Custom House Plaza, near the harbor in historic downtown Monterey, the Winemakers' Celebration draws crowds for tasting from over 40 Monterey County wineries accompanied by live music, great food and educational exhibits. Attendees can view demonstrations of barrel making, and chat with the winemakers and others in a relaxed, casual and fun atmosphere. The Celebration is usually held in mid-August.

Passport Weekend gives participants the opportunity to sample wines at several of Monterey County's 20 tasting rooms, getting a personalized passport stamped at each stop. After gathering stamps, participants are eligible for winery related prizes. Held in February, the Passport Weekend is a great way to explore Monterey Wine Country.

The future looks very bright indeed for the Monterey County wine industry. Vintners and growers continue to experiment with growing techniques such as trellising that take advantage and capitalize on the raw ingredients that nature has provided. New varietals are tested, and more and more acreage is being given over to wine grape production. And the winemakers and growers have banded together to form the Monterey County Vintners and Growers Association to share information and to promote and support the art and science of wine to the public at large. Already a well-regarded producing area among those in the know, Monterey County — and the wines produced here — promise to take a place among the great wine regions of the world.

—Michael Chatfield

The Synergy of Winemaking . . .

. . . Most farmers would look at this soil and cringe. It's not even soil, really. More like a field of rocks with some dirt between them to keep them from grinding together. But to Rick Boyer, this land is rich with possibilities. This is where he grows the grapes that will become the exceptional wines of Jekel Vineyards.

Those rocks—"Greenfield potatoes"—are fist-sized chunks of granite, wrestled by the fantastic power of the Arroyo Seco River from their birthplace miles upstream. They come to rest here in Jekel's Sanctuary Estate Vineyard. The stones lucky enough to be on the surface soak up the heat of the day, retaining and radiating the sun's essence far into the cool evening.

This vineyard is in the shadow of the Santa Lucias, the mountains that define the western edge of the Salinas Valley. In a ravine carved out by the Arroyo Seco, the land is sheltered from the howling, hot daytime winds of the Salinas

Valley, but the gentle, cool winds from the Monterey Bay are channeled here during the evening. This combination of soil, warm days and cool evenings conspires to naturally stress the vines, and force the roots to grow deep. The result? Fewer, smaller grapes with concentrated and complex flavors and characteristics.

It's well known that fine wine results when the vines suffer. But that doesn't mean that they're neglected: quite the contrary. Since he believes that "flavor is developed in the vineyard," a complex, sometimes subtle dance is performed to achieve the perfect balance to which Rick Boyer aspires. One aspect of the quest is immediately apparent in the rows of vines at the Sanctuary and

Gravelstone Vineyards. Every seventh row throughout the vineyard, the usually tidy space between vines is a tangle of wildflowers and what looks like . . . weeds? This is no accident. Each plant in that "cover crop" has been carefully chosen for its ability to attract, feed or shelter the complex universe of insects and other pests that inhabit and threaten the growth of the precious vines. "We are trying to create an environment on the ground where both the predators and the prey can exist and create a balance with each other," says Boyer. It's an ongoing battle for control with the prize being the fruit of those vines — the raw material for the Jekel family of varietal wines — Cabernet Sauvignon, Chardonnay, Riesling, Pinot Noir and others.

Growing techniques practiced at Jekel are organic, but not for marketing reasons. For Rick, the term organic is a philosophical platform, one that defines how people at Jekel work together—and how they work on and with the earth.

Synergy is defined as "the combined power of a group of things when they are working together which is greater than the total power achieved by each working separately," and, although wordy, that definition pretty much sums up the approach at Jekel. For example, in addition to the aforementioned plants between the rows, a flock of chickens can be seen pecking among the vines. What role could chickens possibly play in the production of fine wine? Ask Rick.

"The chickens are a new experiment," Rick says. "They feed on the cover crops, and we get the eggs." That makes sense, as people need a good breakfast for the long days required at a winery, especially during the crush. But these eggs are used for "fining," an ancient, common process in which egg whites (other winemakers use milk, clay or activated charcoal) are introduced to the wine in the barrel to remove proteins and other particles that could cloud the finished product. All traces of the egg are removed prior to bottling.

Rick Boyer is one of Monterey County's most respected winemakers. Youthful, inquisitive and articulate, he clearly loves his work; loves experimenting with new ideas and techniques and measuring the results. Rick has the mind of a scientist and the heart of an activist, and he exudes an intense respect for the environment. When not at the vineyards, he raises Bonsai trees as a hobby. "With Bonsai, you've got life in a confined area," he says. "And you get to create a world with it." That sums up his approach to the Jekel properties: recently he planted dozens of olive trees around the Sanctuary vineyard, along with plots of daffodils and other flowers. While wine growers care about little but the next year's harvest, Rick is thinking far beyond that—the olives testify to that, since it can take at least seven years before an olive tree bears fruit.

Described as a "veritable sleeper that just goes quietly about its business of making better wine with each vintage," Jekel Vineyards has a promising future indeed. And it deserves its place as a very bright star of the Monterey County wine scene.

— Michael Chatfield

Sun...sea

Bathed by the Sun, Touched by the Sea. . .

. . . On a stunningly beautiful spring morning, a light breeze from the ocean ruffling his hair, Chuck Wagner sifts the loose Mer Soleil Vineyard soil through his fingers. He is deep into an explanation of why he chose to plant Chardonnay here in the Santa Lucia Highlands of Salinas Valley when he kneels to pick a tiny plant. "Pineapple weed," he says. Sure enough, the sweet aroma of that tropical fruit greets the nose.

This is a man of the earth. A farmer. "Frankly, I can't imagine a better way of life than growing grapes," he says. After all, when all the glamour of the wine industry, all the hoopla, all the flowery language is put aside, winemaking still begins with agriculture—man asking the earth and the elements to do his bidding. Chuck is one of California's most respected vintners. And the nose that found the pineapple among the weeds is a finely calibrated instrument, easily capable of finding the distinctive fragrance of a tropical fruit in the least likely place.

Chuck's son Charlie never had to grapple with the career choice dilemma familiar to many young people. From a tender age, he worked in and around the vineyards and winery at Caymus, the family flagship at Rutherford in the Napa Valley. It is easy to believe that wine flows through this quintessentially Californian young man's veins. He began working at Mer Soleil before he was old enough to drive and already has more than a decade of experience here.

Under Chuck's tutelage, Charlie has evolved into the winemaker at Mer Soleil, while his father focuses on the vineyard. The easy, familiar relationship between father and son is overlaid with that of mentor and apprentice. They share a passion for making the finest wine possible. "We're not interested in making mediocre wines," Chuck says.

The Wagner family has been making wine in California since the turn of the last century. The Wagner forefathers immigrated to the Bay Area from Alsace in 1885 and purchased farmland in Rutherford following the 1906 San Francisco earthquake. By Prohibition, the family was producing 30,000 gallons of bulk wine per year. In 1941, having survived the "noble experiment," Chuck's parents, Charlie Wagner and Lorna Belle Glos Wagner, purchased their own Rutherford land. They immediately planted some grapevines and were well regarded as growers and home winemakers for three decades.

In 1972, Charlie, Lorna and their then 21-year-old son Chuck founded Caymus Vineyards. More than 60 acres of Cabernet Sauvignon remain the core of Caymus, widely considered one of California's finest labels. Chuck took control of winemaking in 1984 and has since garnered numerous awards and accolades for his Cabernets.

Then, in the late 1980s, Chuck was drawn to the Salinas Valley, believing that the soil and climate here were perfectly suited to the Chardonnay he envisioned. In 1988, he planted the first of what would eventually grow to be 550 acres on the slopes of the Sierra de Salinas mountains that define the western boundary of the valley. The initial planting was of Chardonnay, the variety which established the independent Mer Soleil brand. Later, small amounts of Viognier, Marsanne, Roussanne and Pinot Noir were added in selected areas. The first bottling of Mer Soleil Chardonnay, from the 1992 vintage, was released in 1995.

Based on what is best suited to each vineyard block's topography, soil type, drainage, and exposure to sun and wind, Chuck has made choices in the direction the rows of vines are oriented, the type and timing of irrigation, and the trellis systems used to support the vines. The results take advantage of all the differing characteristics of the land. His latest innovation is a trellis called "trentina," which slants the vines toward the sun for maximum morning exposure while offering afternoon protection of the fruit.

Once the fruit is harvested, Charlie crushes and ferments each of the nine Chardonnay clones used in Mer Soleil separately, increasing the choices available to him later. Fermentation takes place in oak barrels, most of them French, but Charlie selects the barrels from a number of coopers. "I want to have as many layers of flavor as I can when I make the final blend," he explains. Depending upon the vintage, some barrels of wine may undergo malolactic (or "secondary") fermentation, a

process that can impart a buttery note to the wine and add complexity. The barrels rest in an immaculate small building on the property that boasts a stunning view of the valley below. The winery is a strictly workmanlike production facility. It is not open to the public and has no tasting or sales room.

Mer Soleil translates literally as "sea and sun,"

and both elements are key to the wine made here. Monterey Bay is just 16 miles from the vineyard and its influence is keenly felt. And the sun is what has made the Salinas Valley one of the most valuable agricultural areas in the world.

During the growing season, the typical day goes like this: by daybreak, cooling tendrils of fog have infiltrated the entire length of the Salinas Valley. Here at the northern end of the Highlands, the fog clears early, allowing the sun to begin heating the air. By noon, the fog is a memory, as the sun shimmers across the vines. In the afternoon, winds—called "howlers"—rush from the mouth of the Valley southward, tempering the sun's heat. Towards evening, the thick fog of the bay can be seen looming in the northwestern sky as it begins its slow re-encroachment. The day's heat quickly dissipates under the moisture of the fog. This pattern of alternating sun and cooling fog is responsible for balancing Mer Soleil Chardonnay's deeply ripe tropical flavors and refreshing acidity.

This cycle also provides for an exceptionally long growing season, the harvest typically taking place in November after the grape clusters have turned a deep golden color. The southern-facing side of the vines is usually harvested first, and the northern side is picked up to two weeks later. The lush, full-bodied style of the resulting wine has been praised by critics and wine lovers alike since the first vintage.

27

A few years ago, Chuck planted 100 acres of Meyer lemons upwind of the vines. Whether or not the presence of lemons enhances the inherent citrusy quality of the wine is an open question, but it is intriguing and somewhat romantic to think so. The bushy lemon trees provide a striking contrast to the marching rows of vines, and they do fill the air with the tang of citrus. The lemons are sold to a local fruit broker.

Charlie and Chuck have long had an interest in fine dessert wines, and from the 2000 vintage Charlie made a late-harvest white wine, called LATE, from grapes affected by *Botrytis cinerea.* An organism that causes grapes to shrivel and therefore concentrate

their flavor and sugar, *Botrytis* can spoil wine grapes if it occurs too early in the growing season. But when it descends at the right time, truly great dessert wines can be made from the affected grapes, which are harvested as late as mid-December. "Hardly anyone would believe that this clear, sweet wine could be made from such dark, shriveled grapes," says Charlie, "but it's worth the wait and the effort."

For the next generation of Wagners and their wines, it's a foregone conclusion that the family's commitment to excellence will carry on. Says Chuck: "We want to make extremely good wines here in the Santa Lucia Highlands—that's what Mer Soleil stands for."

—Michael Chatfield

FANDANGO RESTAURANT

Cuisine of the sun . . .

. . . Excellence occurs when talented people commit their lives to the pursuit of a singular ideal. Hard work, dedication and experience hone excellence into the fine edge of artistry. Pierre and Marietta Bain, proprietors, have sculpted the Fandango experience into a work of restaurant art, where the act of dining transcends ordinary and transports guests into an ethereal world of pure artistic restaurant expression.

Perched midway up the 17th Street hill in picturesque Pacific Grove, this European country-style farm house beckons regulars and newcomers alike, singing out its sensory serenade of warm colors, earthy textures, alluring aromas, smiling faces and simple, yet sophisticated selections. Everything at Fandango is done the way it has always been done throughout the world at all the best establishments—a direct result of Pierre Bain's upbringing.

For nearly three centuries, the Bain family has been at the helm of the Grand Hotel Bain in Provence, where, from birth, Pierre was taught the fine techniques of old world food preparation, humble, sincere customer service and unyielding commitment to quality. At Fandango, these traditions are rigorously adhered to by a loyal, long-tenured staff of talented and dedicated professionals.

Dining at Fandango in one of the five individually appointed dining rooms makes you feel as though you are visiting a homey, European country house, where friendly, welcoming family cater to your every whim, then ply you with fantastic homemade delicacies, elegant wines, scrumptious freshly-baked desserts and unlimited hospitality.

From the moment you enter the spacious parking lot and soak in the comforting visual splendor of the restaurant's exterior, the Fandango charm casts its spell upon you. Inside, gracious, caring service will sooth and encourage as you peruse the tantalizing menu of Mediterranean specialties such as Bouillabaisse, Osso Buco, Paella, Rack of Lamb or Roasted Duckling. At Fandango, each delicacy is prepared using only the freshest ingredients, always from scratch, the old-world way.

Choose from an abundant, award-winning wine list that represents all the important wine-producing regions of the world. With over 1,000 selections, there is certainly something for everyone, and the friendly, knowledgeable staff will happily guide you throughout the dining experience to ensure your utmost satisfaction. You can always enlist the assistance of Pierre or Marietta, both of whom actively participate in daily service.

32

An upstairs addition, complete with its own duplicate kitchen, provides the perfect party atmosphere for gatherings of up to fifty people. As with the main floor dining rooms, the décor reflects Pierre and Marietta's European influence, gentile elegance and limitless hospitality. Fresh flowers, a recurring theme throughout Fandango, join cascading natural light, beautiful potted plants, authentic decorations and warm, cozy materials like stone, wood and stucco.

Sunday Brunch, a Monterey Peninsula favorite, showcases the glass-enclosed main dining room, complete with its own warming stone fireplace. Along with great food and friendly service, daily lunch patrons get to experience the alluring charm of Fandango's architecture and design during daylight, when the natural shifting light casts delicate shadows, changing scenes throughout the restaurant.

Dinner is a show unto itself as Fandango's well-rehearsed staff dances the dance of its namesake. Hosts and waiters gracefully move around and through the dining rooms while cooks and crewmembers fandango in the heat of the kitchen, all to the ever changing beat created by each night's special configuration of guests, who provide the pulse, the rhythm of this magical dance.

Join Pierre and Marietta Bain in Fandango. Let your senses dance to the artistry of a lifetime's dedication to your enjoyment. There is going out to eat, then there is Fandango.

— Ray Napolitano

VENTANA VINEYARDS AND MEADOR ESTATE

Creating Fine Wine in the Vineyard . . .

. . . Full of character. Robust and earthy. Expressive and memorable. Complex yet approachable. These words describe winegrower and innovator Doug Meador as much as they do the wines he entices from his vineyards. To Doug, the titles *winegrower* and *winemaker* are synonymous, consistent with his long-held belief that "fine wine is created in the vineyard." The estate bottled wines of Ventana Vineyards and Meador Estate are masterfully created in his 400-acre vineyard in Monterey County's Arroyo Seco AVA.

In stark contrast to textbook, carved-in-stone methods of making wine, Meador prefers the seamlessly integrated roles of shepherd and "mad scientist," a title favored by wife and business partner LuAnn Meador. "We enjoy what we do, guiding and caring for the vines, working within the limits of what mother Monterey County gave us," says Doug. "If the grapes arrive at the winery in proper condition, winemaking is babysitting."

A passionate pursuer of the "what ifs?," Doug Meador approaches winegrowing as he does life — fueled by curiosity. Following his years as a Navy jet pilot and with a degree in econometrics from the University of Washington, he was destined to join the family apple growing business in Washington state. In the early '70s, he helped fund a group of friends in planting 2,500 acres of wine grapes in the Salinas Valley, and his curiosity got the better of him. Captured by the challenges of growing fine wine grapes in the arid-by-day, chilly-by-night, windy and rocky conditions that characterize Arroyo Seco, he purchased 300 acres of what he considered to be the best of the original lot. He christened it Ventana — meaning "window" in Spanish — as it afforded a view of the Ventana Wilderness and a vision of Monterey County as one of the great wine regions of the world.

At a time when many in the industry ascribed to the theory that a higher grape yield translated to lower quality, he set out to discover the real truth for himself. Using the vineyard as his laboratory, Doug conducted experiments with every aspect of the growing process, from the design of the trellis system and the clonal vines best suited to the environment to vine and row spacing, and pruning, trimming and harvesting techniques. Disproving the less-is-better-theory, he planted vines closer together in an innovative, vertical formation that enabled him to triple and quadruple tonnage per acre while noticeably

improving the quality. To this day, his grapes are purchased and prized by makers of other award-winning California wines as well as being showcased under his Ventana Vineyards and Meador Estate labels.

After more than a decade of discoveries that moved the Monterey County wine industry light-years forward, Doug decided to expand his laboratory from the inside out. Understanding that several unique "terroirs" — a term that encompasses soil, microclimate, wind exposure and other growing conditions — existed within his vineyard, he carefully matched the varietal to its ideal terroir and winemaking techniques, creating sections or "blocks" in which he conducted various studies. Meador Estate wines, first brought to market in the late 1990s, are the fruits of this tinkering. His Syrah, aptly named "Maverick" — largely because it's a little more consumer friendly than "Mad Scientist,"— has already drawn applause from the international wine community. At the 2003 Vinalies Internationales, Vins du Monde, Denologues de France in Paris, Meador brought home the gold (Vinalies d'Or) for his 1998 Meador Estate "Maverick" Syrah.

The list of "firsts" attributed to Doug Meador is as long as the

"legs" on his wines. First to correctly identify clonal vines that had been previously mismatched with the county's growing conditions. First to introduce malolactic fermentation to the making of white wines in America. First in the U.S. to practice basal leaf removal to increase air flow and allow the sun to influence the sweetness of the grapes, a technique traced back to ancient Greek viticulturists. And first to plant French barrel oak trees in this country.

A fan of fruit forward wine with ever-so-subtle touches of oak, Doug carefully selects the barrels for his wine. And, of course, he experiments with type and origins of the oak to achieve specific characteristics in each vintage. "We like to think of oak as a way to frame the "window," says Doug. "Primarily, we use French oak barrels and those grown and crafted in Minnesota. We look for tight grain in the wood to achieve only a hint of oak so the fruit can be enjoyed and appreciated."

While experimentation and change are second nature to Meador, his wines enjoy extraordinary consistency in quality and character, due in part to the longevity of the core winemaking team. Since 1997, Reggie Hammond has overseen the vineyard and winemaking operations as director of production. This "family" owned winery is one of the "extended" variety where members, by blood or kinship, invest of themselves in this labor of love. The Ventana Vineyards label itself is richly

expressive with family symbolism including three deltas, one for each of their children and the double-tailed cat, the insignia on the jet Doug flew for the Navy.

In 1984, Doug married LuAnn, a local banking executive whom he credits with not only raising awareness of his labels but also those of Monterey County's many small and mid-sized wineries. LuAnn runs the marketing end of the business and has been instrumental in putting the Ventana and Meador Estate wines on the world map, and on countless tables around the globe. She's also a familiar face on the county's wine scene having served as President of the Monterey County Vintner's and Growers Association (MCVGA) in 1999 and 2000. In 1997, she founded and chaired "The Great Wine Escape Weekend" for the MCVGA and also in 1997 she was presented the "Hospitality Professional of the Year" award from the Monterey County Hospitality Association. Luann is also active on many other leadership boards in Monterey County.

"Wine is a wonderful way to explore cultures and traditions, both by growing it and by enjoying it" says LuAnn. "It's also a way to express the creativity, skill, and in our case, the inquisitiveness of the winemaker. Our vacations tend to focus on visiting other countries and exploring their winemaking techniques as well as their heritage and way of life."

"When it comes right down to it," says Doug, "we enjoy producing wines that people love to drink — wines that are a good value and express the true character of each grape varietal. Wine and food are meant to be fun for people to enjoy and we love creating foods and testing them with our wines and the many other incredible vintages we discover along the way."

While there's no knighting for the winemaker, Doug Meador has plenty of medals, awards and accolades to proclaim the success of his experiments. In fact, Ventana Vineyards is the "most award-winning single vineyard in America." Keep in mind that many of the awards not only recognize the quality of his vintages compared to other California and U.S. wines, but those grown in some of the oldest and most renowned regions of France, Italy and other major wine producing nations.

"Life at the vineyard has to be lived 20 years in the future," says Doug, "meaning that we have to plant now for the types of wine we anticipate consumers will want 20 years from now. And the quest is part of the reward. We're always searching for new and ancient ways to influence the character of our wines. The experiment never ends."

—Melanie Belon Chatfield

Fine Dining

A Beautifully Orchestrated Icon of Fine Dining . . .

. . . Immortalized in John Steinbeck's *Cannery Row,* this area of Monterey was once the center of the sardine fishing and canning industries. Tired of the productivity lost to tardy post-lunch-break cannery employees, owners established a cafeteria for their workers just one block up from the Row. It was in this building that Ted Balestreri and Bert Cutino opened the 72-seat Sardine Factory Restaurant on October 2, 1968, and inspired what today is the heart of Monterey's bustling hospitality industry.

From humble beginnings and with pure ingenuity and tenacity, Ted and Bert grew the Sardine Factory into an icon of fine dining. The restaurant is renowned for service that closely approximates "the royal treatment," sans the necessity of blue blood. It is known and remembered for inventive, yet recognizable cuisine that relies heavily on fresh seafood and prime meats. And its legendary wine program has earned the Sardine Factory the *Wine Spectator* Grand Award for one of the Best Wine Lists in the World every year since 1982.

When Ted and Bert opened the doors, the wine list was largely determined by their spirits distributor, who doubled as a "wine consultant." As the restaurant grew to its current capacity of 220, the wine list followed suit. "The development and growth of the restaurant and our wine program closely parallel the evolution of California's wine industry and the emergence of Monterey County as a major wine producing region," says Ted. "Today, some of our most popular wines are from Monterey County."

It was a young employee by the name of Fred Dame who really got the wine barrel rolling. He initiated the restaurant's formal wine program in 1982, and it now features more than 1,000 labels and 30,000 bottles. Ted Balestreri conceived the idea of a wine cellar to serve as a unique private dining facility and to house their expanding collection. As Bert, Ted, then Banquet Manager Craig Clark and Fred described the ideal banquet room, the design of the Wine Cellar was first put to paper through sketches by artist Roy Ami Hamlin. Craig then built the Wine Cellar himself. As eclectic as an art museum with a collection that spans hundreds of years, the room is decorated with beautifully married styles from the eras of Napoleon III, Queen Victoria and Louis XIV.

Seating 28 people at a table hewn from a fallen Big Sur redwood, the wine cellar hosts private dining spectaculars where everything is carefully choreographed from start to finish. Today, Wine Cellar host Giovanni Sercia and Executive Chef Robert Mancuso team up to orchestrate each event, matching the flavors and intensity levels of the cuisine and wine to classical music pieces: A little Vivaldi with foie gras and grilled abalone, moving through the courses to filet mignon and Wagner. For the final course, Giovanni typically chooses a musical piece related in some way to the group. "There are limits however," he cautions. "We have to stop at Willie Nelson tunes."

Ted beams when he tells the story of how Fred brought home England's Krug Cup after earning the highest score in the history of the world-renowned Master Sommelier tasting exam. It was the first time the Cup had left England and a BBC reporter was quoted as saying, "Oh my God, he's an American."

In its 21-year history, the Sardine Factory's wine program has known only three Cellar Masters — the aforementioned Fred, Andrea Fulton, one of several female sommeliers in the restaurant and one of the few female Cellar Masters in the country, and Marc Cutino, who has been Cellar Master since 2000. Marc, brother Bart, Ted Balestreri II and his brother Vincent are members of the second generation, carrying on the business traditions of the first generation. Bart Cutino has been an Assistant Manager at the Sardine Factory since 2000; the younger Ted was in management at the restaurant for five years before taking on the role of Director of Hospitality & Lodging for Restaurants Central. Vincent works as a Project Manager for Restaurants Central and serves as "consumer advocate" at the restaurant. "Vincent loves dining here and 'representing' the customer's point of view," Ted says with a smile.

At its very core, The Sardine Factory is all about people and ensuring that they have a one-of-a-kind, not-to-be-forgotten experience. "We want people to enjoy themselves and celebrate," says Ted, who does whatever it takes to create a festive atmosphere. Growing up, he was taught the etiquette of the time—to uncork the wine as discreetly as possible. "I thought it should be the opposite," says Ted. "I wanted people to hear the cork coming out of the bottle and look around to see others truly enjoying themselves. So I would accentuate the popping sound with my lips. We had the loudest uncorkings in town."

As one can expect from one of the "Best Wine Lists in the World" for 21 years running, some of the world's most prestigious and priciest vintages appear here—including a Chateau Lafite Rothschild Pauillac 1870 that goes for a mere $10,000. Pleasantly surprising, however, are the equally impressive, yet accessibly priced wines that are featured daily as *Selections from the Cellar Master*. There are more than two dozen choices—reds and whites, domestic and imported—and nothing over $30.

When asked for the name of his favorite wine, Ted smiles and answers with the utmost diplomacy, "My favorite wine is the last memorable wine I had with a great meal, and it probably came from California, most likely enjoyed with friends from Monterey County."

—Melanie Belon Chatfield

HAMES VALLEY VINEYARDS

Beauty, Power and Grace . . .

. . . Hames Valley Vineyards lies in a basin of gentle, undulating hills fenced in by steeper, higher ridges—not quite mountains, not quite hills. There's a big-sky feeling not found in most parts of Monterey County and neighbors are widely spaced.

Bob and Shelley Denney have been growing wine grapes for more than 25 years now, first for others, then as consultants, and finally as owners of Hames Valley Vineyards, located in the extreme southern end of the county. "When we came here, we really felt tied to the land," recalls Shelley. "It called to us."

Locating here was not an altogether emotional decision for the couple. The earth of the Hames Valley American Viticultural Area (AVA) is composed of shaly loam, a soil type that doesn't retain water particularly well. That makes it ideal for the balance of nurture and stress that vintners strive for when growing fine wine grapes.

The influence of the Monterey Bay is much less predominant here, and the valley is sheltered from the winds that howl through the Salinas Valley to the north — ideal conditions in which to grow premium red wine grapes. During the height of the growing season the day/night temperature differential can be as much as 50 degrees. The heat of the day allows the grapes to achieve their full potential of flavor and ripeness. "Every year is a vintage year here," says Bob.

The Denneys were instrumental in obtaining the American Viticultural Area (AVA) designation for the Hames Valley, which was granted in 1994. They felt that the growing conditions in the valley were unique from those in the larger Monterey AVA, and that the grapes grown in its warmer climate were distinctive and worthy of a separate designation.

For generations before the Denneys arrived, this land was used for cattle grazing and growing barley, a sturdy crop used to feed livestock. It was subsistence farming, the type that could just barely sustain a family. Enter Bob and Shelley. In 1988 they purchased the first 630 acres of what would eventually become the 2,400-acre Hames Valley Vineyards Ranch. Being good stewards of the land is a high priority in this family. Cattle are fenced off to prevent damage to the native oak trees, wetlands have been restored and thousands of acorns have been seeded throughout the

48

property in an effort to restore the habitat. The land has been graded for maximum efficiency with minimum impact.

Over time, the Denney family had become friendly with a man who had lived and farmed on this land for most of his life. He had subsequently moved away, but one day he arrived with his car's trunk loaded with boxes. They contained early ranch artifacts and fossils that he had collected on the ranch over the years and had taken with him. "These belong here," he said, "and you are the kind of people who would appreciate them." Today, they are treasured and respected as part of the

vital history of the land with which the Denneys have been entrusted.

Right out of college, Bob made wine in a rustic old redwood winery on property he was managing in the Santa Clara Valley. It was a long road from that first hobby bottling to the premium wines produced by the Denneys today. The couple managed vineyards in the Central Valley for many years, and then formed a farm management company in 1985. Most of the grapes grown in that region are destined for relatively inexpensive, mass-produced wines. But they were interested in growing grapes for—and eventually producing—premium, high-quality wines to rival those coming from the great wine regions of the world.

Only the cream of their crop—the finest 2 percent of the 700 acres of grapes grown here—are used for the Hames Valley label. Customers of the rest of the crop are a Who's Who of the California wine business. Growing throughout the property are Cabernet Sauvignon, Merlot, Cabernet Franc and Syrah. Blocks of Zinfandel, Petite Verdot, Sauvignon Blanc and Viognier are also here.

This is a thoroughly 21st century operation. Remote weather monitoring sensors are situated throughout the vineyard, providing real-time data to a computer that, combined with frequent plant and soil testing, helps in calculating optimum irrigation schedules. The Hames Valley receives an average of only 10 to 12 inches of rainfall per year, making precise water management critical.

The first commercial wines released by Hames Valley Vineyards were a limited quantity of just 2000 vintage Cabernet Sauvignon and a Syrah. The 2001 wines, a Cabernet, a Merlot, and a Cabernet Franc were released in June 2003

and are available in larger quantities. The 2000 Cabernet is excellent, with classic black cherry and cassis notes and has proven to be a favorite of consumers and critics alike. In their first wine competition the Hames Valley 2001 Merlot received a gold medal at the 2003 L.A. County Fair. This release bodes well for the future of the Hames Valley label.

Bob has a passion for building things. Starting with that original 630 acres, he, Shelley and their three daughters have grown Hames Valley into a 2,400-acre ranch, a thriving operation that now employs more than a dozen people. But it's not all grapes.

The Denneys are California's largest breeders of registered Percheron draft horses which are elegant, stately, thoroughly majestic 2,000 pound creatures originally imported from France in the 19th Century. For many years, Percherons did America's heavy lifting, providing muscle for farm work and pulling wagons filled with goods and people across the land. Mechanization has replaced the draft horse in modern times, but there is a thriving draft horse industry in the country today. The Denneys started with one Percheron several years ago and now more than 50 of these magnificent creatures call Hames Valley home, including 12 new foals. A Percheron named Classy graces the wine label, and the family has a collection of antique wagons that are shown at fairs and events all over the country. A team of six Percheron mares serves as impressive ambassadors of Hames Valley Vineyards wines.

But most importantly, what has taken root at Hames Valley Vineyards is a closely-knit farming family that embodies values rarely seen in more urban environments. The Denney's three daughters all share the family passion and sense of commitment. Amy is studying for her Masters at the Yale Divinity School and will become an Episcopal priest, Robin is studying viticulture, wine making and political science at the University of California at Davis, and Audrey is a leader at the state and national level with the Future Farmers of America.

Audrey began overseeing the ranch's livestock operation at the age of 12. A successful manager, but also a busy student and FFA leader, she saw the enterprise grow beyond the point at which she had time to run it. An employee was hired to take things from there. Committed to the family business, she will enroll at U.C. Davis to study animal science and management. Robin is planning to return to the ranch after graduating to oversee the grape growing and winemaking operation. She is very interested in the political aspects of the agriculture industry and has served internships with lawmakers in Sacramento and Washington, D.C. to gain experience with the legislative process. All the girls are interested in maintaining their connection to this land and in helping others to be formed by connecting to the earth through agriculture.

The wine produced by Hames Valley Vineyards is currently being made by winemaker Christian Roguenant at Orcutt Road Cellars in San Luis Obispo. With 25 years experience in growing wine grapes the Denneys are purposely taking the making of premium wines slowly, in order to get it just right.

Currently, the vineyard is not open to the public, but there are plans afoot for a visitor's center on the ranch. There the Denneys would be able to exhibit two passions simultaneously: Percherons and wine. Then the public at large will be able to witness first hand the beauty, the power, the grace, the passion and commitment that this family has brought to this lovely little valley in Monterey County.

—Michael Chatfield

Showcase

A Showcase of Fine Wines . . .

. . . What began as a place to showcase the fine wines of Monterey County's seven American Viticultural Areas (AVAs) has become the "capital" of Monterey County wine country. Designated as The Official Regional Wine Visitors' Center, *A Taste of Monterey* is akin to a wine lover's museum.

Housed in a renovated circa 1918 sardine cannery, the flagship tasting room on Monterey's Cannery Row allows one to bask in the history of the place as well as the decades-long heritage of the many wineries represented there. An entire wall of windows overlooks the magnificent Monterey Bay, providing a stunning backdrop for a wine tasting adventure.

It all started in 1993 when Ken and Robyn Rauh were recruited by a group of Monterey County vineyard owners to establish a unique regional wine tasting and education center. Each had more than a decade of experience in the industry and neither was a stranger to the area or the prominence it had

rightfully gained as a world-class wine region. Robyn was raised on a ranch in the Salinas Valley where the entire family participated in planting vineyards. During and after college in Southern California, where she and Ken met, she assisted in building both national and tasting room sales for Chateau Julien Wine Estate in Carmel Valley. Ken worked in the tasting room of Paul Masson Winery and served as a tour guide for The Monterey Vineyard.

Working cooperatively with the Monterey County Vintners and Growers Association, Ken and Robyn launched what has become a popular destination with tourists as well as local wine connoisseurs. Given that all but one of the county's AVAs are located in the Salinas Valley, Salinas was the logical choice for a second location that opened in 2000 next door to the National Steinbeck Center.

From its inception, A Taste of Monterey has been more than a tasting room and wine shop. Directors and staff proudly assume the mantle of "Monterey County Wine Ambassador" and promote the bounty of the region through educational exhibits, seminars, a mobile wine tasting program, a nationwide wine club and a popular website.

"It's impossible to separate winegrowing and winemaking from the history of Monterey County and its people," says Ken Rauh. "Vineyards were first planted here in the 18th century. Today, our vintners gracefully blend old-world traditions with the best of modern winemaking techniques. Robyn and I enjoy sharing what we know about Monterey County and its wines, and we learn something new every day."

When Bobbie Flay, celebrity chef and host of the Food Network's Food Nation series, decided to feature Monterey in an episode, Ken was called on to present and pair the area's wines with local cuisine. It was a natural fit and A Taste of Monterey had its debut on national television. "We are so

proud of our area's heritage and the unique foods and wines that reflect the many cultures that call Monterey County home," says Ken. "It was fun to work with Bobby Flay and see how taken he was with the whole experience."

Thanks to the innovation and intuitiveness of Ken and Robyn, the fruits of Monterey County's vines are accessible through the Monterey Wine Club that now has more than 2,400 members nationwide. "The Wine Club is our way of introducing people to a greater variety of our county's wines," explains Ken. "It's impractical for a person to try more than a few wines during a visit to our tasting rooms. So the Wine Club lets members sample and learn about a new wine each month. We think it's important for members to not only know about the wine, but the winemakers who craft each vintage."

Captivating vistas of the Monterey Bay, intriguing viticulture exhibits and a well-schooled staff, complemented by a crisp sauvignon blanc or a full-bodied merlot, promise a multi-sensory experience at A Taste of Monterey.

–Melanie Belon Chatfield

CHALONE VINEYARD

A Dream of wines to rival the best. . .

. . . East of the Salinas Valley, a little south of Soledad, in a remote segment of the Gavilan Mountain Range near the extinct volcanic peaks now known as Pinnacles National Monument, Chalone Vineyard majestically occupies a few hundred acres of land once roamed by the Chollen or Chalone tribe of the Costanoan Indians.

At 1800 feet of elevation, the sparse, limestone-rich soil and dry climate at the foot of the basalt Pinnacles help Chalone Vineyard produce wines of distinctive character, depth and complexity. Temperatures can range from highs of 90 degrees at midday to as low as 50 degrees at night during most of the growing season. Soils high in calcareous rock and decomposed granite reduce vigor in vines, naturally limiting crop loads and contributing to even ripening.

These unique characteristics are what first drew a Frenchman named Charles Tamm, who planted a small vineyard in 1919. He was followed by William and Agnes Silvear in 1946, winemaker Philip Togni, who produced the first wine to bear the Chalone Vineyard label in 1960, then Dick Graff. Graff recognized similarities in the soil between Chalone Vineyard and the Burgundy region in France and believed that world class Chardonnay and Pinot Noir could be produced here using the same techniques the French had employed for centuries.

In 1976, at the famous Paris tasting held by Steven Spurrier, the California wines trounced their French counterparts, jumpstarting world wide acceptance of the state as a world-class wine producing region. Chalone Chardonnay was there, placing third, ahead of all but one of the French Burgundies. Chalone and California were on their way.

In those earlier years, farming Chalone Vineyard was especially difficult. Water had to be trucked in from miles away and power was supplied by generators, yet the effort proved more than worth it. Chalone's reputation for creating beautiful, distinct Chardonnay, Pinot Noir, Pinot Blanc and Chenin Blanc steadily grew, due in large part to the vineyard's most outstanding characteristic, its individually unique expression of *terroir* — the essence of the grape's qualities as a direct result of where it grows.

Characterized by its signature minerality and brioche, the area upon which Chalone Vineyard is planted was awarded its own AVA, or American Viticultural Area. An area may only be designated such when it proves to be completely different than that of its surroundings. This designation further distinguished Chalone Vineyard as being truly unique.

In 1984, Chalone once again helped pioneer the industry, becoming the first publicly traded wine company. Since then, folks who hold at least 100 shares of Chalone Wine Group stock meet yearly at Chalone Vineyard for its unparalleled Shareholders Celebration where they enjoy spectacular wines, a delicious luncheon, magnificent views and warm, convivial socializing with other shareholders.

The goal at Chalone has always been to create world-class wines that uniquely express the characteristics of their grapes' origin, without compromise and with unyielding dedication to quality and improvement.

60

Four years of vineyard additions and modifications to the Chardonnay have recently been completed, culminating in greater homogeneity of ripeness.

In 1997 Chalone began to revamp the Pinot Noir program by planting Burgundian clones not readily available in the United States. The resultant bottlings are proving to be richer, denser and darker than those of the past decade.

Chalone Vineyard Syrah, planted on a southern-facing section of the vineyard, forms its own little Cote-Rotie. Using traditional techniques of 100% estate grapes aged in French barrels along with the blending of tiny amounts of Viognier and Grenache have led to Chalone Vineyard Syrah rivaling those of the Rhone Valley.

Chalone Vineyard began as a tiny, remote, lone vineyard sight and a dream of wines to rival the best of Burgundy. It has grown into an internationally successful winery committed to perpetuating the original tenets laid down by its founders.

Long, rich tradition combined with progressive, innovative renovation and controlled, thoughtful expansion, have kept Chalone Vineyard at the pinnacle of the wine world. A visit to the beautiful Gavilan Mountain site, confirmed by tastes of the full array of Chalone Vineyard wines will prove to be a wonderful and memorable excursion.

—Ray Napolitano

Harmonious Blending Makes Blackstone Wines Sing . . .

. . . While Blackstone Winery has more then 1,400 acres of vineyards, a winery and a tasting room in Monterey County, Senior Winemaker Dennis Hill likes to think that all California AVAs are potential grape sources for his wines. From Santa Barbara in the south to the Sacramento River Delta in the north, he selects grapes that bring specific characteristics and flavors to each Blackstone vintage. His extensive knowledge of California's AVAs and the style of fruit each produces, combined with his masterful art of blending, have put Blackstone on the road to becoming one of the most popular labels in the country.

"Each growing region has distinct soil, climate and growing conditions that influence the unique characteristics of the fruit," says Dennis, who joined Blackstone in 1994 with more than 20 years of experience tucked neatly under his belt. "Our goal is to create wines that are consistent from vintage to vintage, are approachable and marry nicely with food, yet have a level of complexity to

make them memorable. It's a scientific, artistic melting pot of the best California has to offer." Blackstone's lineup features three varietals that distinctly represent the finest vineyards through-out Monterey County's seven AVAs—Monterey County Sauvignon Blanc, Monterey County Chardonnay and Monterey County Pinot Noir.

The highly-praised wines of Blackstone are a testament to the validity of Hill's winemaking approach. The spicy, peppery characteristics of Monterey County grapes, matched with the richness and complexity of those from Sonoma County and the depth and concentration of flavors of the fruit from Napa Valley create California Cabernet Sauvignon. Eighty-year-old vines near Lodi along with newer vines from coastal Mendocino and inland Paso Robles marry nicely to form the inaugural vintage of Blackstone California Zinfandel.

Blackstone Winery first came to life in 1990 in a "virtual" state. With neither tank nor vineyard, Blackstone contracted with growers and wineries to produce wine under its guidance and label. Within a few years, it became unwieldy to manage the fermentation process at eight wineries dispersed across California's many appellations. At the same time, Dennis desired greater influence over the subtleties of each vintage and was ready to take on new challenges in a single, larger winery.

The wines of Blackstone are the products of ingenuity, artistry and good, long standing partnerships. "The relationships we have with growers around the state are at the core of our wines' success," says Jose Fernandez, CEO and President of Blackstone and its parent company, Pacific Wine Partners. "We work closely with them on pruning, irrigation and harvesting grapes not only for our own wines, but for those sold to other quality vintners."

The company's own 1,400 acres are spread nearly evenly among three Monterey County vineyards and they cover a range of microclimates and growing regions. The cool climate of Vine Del Rey near King City produces Pinot Noir with berry and violet aromas. Coyote Canyon in the San Lucas AVA is a bit warmer with cool rolling hills and sandy soils, yielding lovely blueberry-kissed Merlot. And finally, the Hames Valley AVA, protected from ocean breezes and fog, is home to red wine grapes including Petite Syrah, Malbec and Cabernet Sauvignon.

Expanding on their solid reputation built on Merlot — their signature wine — Blackstone has steadily broadened its repertoire. At this time, that includes seven varietals and three expanding series — Winemaker Select, Prestige Appellation and Reserve. The flagship Merlot varietal tops the list in each of the three series.

"Our focus for the past few years has been on perfecting our portfolio," says Dennis, "with each varietal addressing a particular style, flavor and price range."

Much to Dennis' delight, Blackstone opened a Sonoma County winery in 2002 where he will focus on expanding their Prestige Appellation and Reserve series of wines. "These two distinct wineries allow our winemaking team to dedicate special attention to each wine within Blackstone's growing portfolio."

Blackstone is part of a family of wineries in the U.S. and also in Australia. "There's a real cross pollination of cultures and winemaking techniques that increases everyone's skills," says Dennis. "My 30-year-and-counting winemaking career has been spent entirely in California. It's exciting to broaden that knowledge with international experience and to have the opportunity to share ideas with winemakers on that continent." The lead winemaker for Blackstone's Monterey County winery, Hugh Reimers, hails from the land Down Under.

As the wines of Blackstone age, are perfected and released, so grow the ever expanding accolades:

"Just when the explosion of new wineries across California seems to quiet down, another producer emerges offering wines too enticing to ignore."
- *Chicago Tribune*

"Although a good inexpensive Merlot is a rarity, this (Blackstone California Merlot) is a happy exception."
- *Food & Wine Magazine*

Blackstone Monterey County Chardonnay took home a Gold Medal from *Jerry Mead's New World International* Wine Com-petition in 2002, and Silver Medals from the *San Francisco Chronicle* Wine Competition in 2002 and 2003.

Winemaker Hill equates fine wine with classical music. "I can listen to the same classical piece many times and still discover something new each time," says Dennis. "It's complex and intriguing, surprising me with nuances and details that I've never heard before. We aim for that same marriage of consistency and discovery in every Blackstone vintage."

—Melanie Belon Chatfield

Unique

Uniquely Flavorful Culinary Creations. . .

. . . Is it possible to find a pearl in a plate of oysters? Passionfish is just such a find. Nestled between the crashing waves of the Pacific and the tranquil waters of the Monterey Bay, Passionfish offers a dining experience that is both rare and exquisite. The combination of Chef Ted Walter's uniquely flavorful culinary creations and an award winning wine list have earned Passionfish a place among California's finest restaurants.

Most are surprised to find this pearl hidden in a non-descript building at the far end of the small Victorian town of Pacific Grove. Others have heard tales of this treasure and search it out. If you are so inclined, the rewards are many.

Once inside, you will immediately come to realize why the owners, Ted and Cindy Walter, coined the name Passionfish. There is a certain jubilance that permeates throughout the restaurant, confirming you're welcome and setting the mood for a fun and relaxing dining experience.

The fresh and simple decor underscores Chef Ted Walter's talents. The four interconnected dining rooms offer intimacy, while the staff's pampering reminds you that you're not at home. You'll find there's something about your server's exuberance that is infectious, for if you listen, jovial conversation and laughter always over shadow the music at Passionfish.

While the atmosphere is casual, Passionfish is hardly frivolous. The Walters are committed to the philosophy of serving

healthy, flavorful, and ecologically sound meal choices. They shop the farmer's markets to select organic produce and purchase sustainable seafood, exclusively. Chef Walter specializes in simple, inspired meals emphasizing the natural flavors of these quality ingredients at their peak of freshness.

Passionfish's ever-changing menu makes each visit a new adventure. If you have an opportunity to sample the Monterey Bay salmon with portobello and pancetta mushroom viniagrette atop house-made potato ravioli, you'll know you have reached heaven. Although the name Passionfish naturally conjures up visions of fresh seafood, the menu always offers many tantalizing alternatives, including prime steaks, fowl, and vegetarian dishes. In fact, Chef Walter's slow-cooked meats, such as roast pork or braised short ribs, are said to be of what legends are made. Many a story of his lamb shanks has been told and retold with starry-eyed remembrance by those who frequent this haven for food and wine aficionados.

Entrees are complemented with Passionfish's unique appetizers, such as the seasonal asparagus fries with red pepper aioli or fresh Monterey Bay calamari with a spicy orange cilantro dipping sauce. Locally grown greens are the foundation for imaginative salads. There's simply nothing like the seductive taste of Chef Walter's fried oyster salad with warm pea shoots and a citrus-soy sauce or the complex flavors of the baked Gorgonzola on curried greens served with a golden chutney.

And the wine flows freely at Passionfish, from a list as diverse as any in the world. Their Wine Spectator award winning wine list offers selections sure to please both the connoisseur and novice alike. Over 300 selections, ranging from local Monterey County varietals to rare and desirable wines from around the world, believe it or not, are all are priced at retail! Chef Walter tastes every wine on the list to ensure it meets the pairing standards of his menu. There simply isn't a bad choice to be found. This leaves you room to be adventurous. Passionfish was recently selected by the National Restaurant Association to receive the prestigious title of "Best Wine List in America."

You may feel slightly forlorn when moving on to dessert, yet the final embrace is just as sweet as your welcome. Choose a delectable dessert fresh from the oven paired with fresh roasted coffee or a selection from the menu of loose leaf teas.

Dining at Passionfish is sure to bring out the passion in you.

Wisdom

A Father's Wisdom, the Son's Lesson . . .

. . . Famed wine writer Hugh Johnson once wrote, "The land itself chooses the crop that suits it best." Jerry Lohr understood this when he selected Monterey's Arroyo Seco appellation as the site for his first vineyard in 1972. One of an illustrious handful of early Monterey winemaking pioneers, J. Lohr Vineyards and Wines has helped redefine the region. Once a relative unknown in the California wine world, Monterey has evolved into one of North America's premier wine growing regions, with Arroyo Seco considered by many to be one of the crown jewels.

A scientist and the son of a South Dakota farming family, Jerry Lohr has combined his two passions in the pursuit of world-class wines. Blending rigorous analytical reasoning with the intuition and hands-on integrity of an artisan farmer, Jerry has spent thirty-two years developing the promise of Monterey. Over the course of those three decades, Jerry grew to be respected as a visionary and a champion of the region. For Jerry, getting his hands dirty

is an integral part of creating exceptional wine and just plain fun. Unrelenting in his pursuit of the most intense flavors, Jerry is active in every facet of winemaking operations, working alongside his hand-picked vineyard team to ensure every viticultural and wine making step — from cultivating the soil to bottling the wine — culminates in wines with the freshest and most vivid flavors.

Nestled against the foothills of the coastal range on gently sloping benchland, the Arroyo Seco property of J. Lohr is uniquely suited for producing rich, sophisticated whites. Unlike red varietals, Chardonnay and Riesling by nature thrive in cool climates with little fluctuation in temperature. When compared with other great Chardonnay regions such as Carneros and the Russian River Valley, Jerry discovered that Arroyo Seco exhibits the lowest daytime average temperature, with the least variation between day and night. Coupled with ideal rocky loam soil, cool afternoon ocean breezes and a remarkably long growing season, J. Lohr's vineyards yield remarkably flavorful and elegant whites year after year.

Jerry attributes most of J. Lohr's success not only to the careful selection and development of the land but to the company's human capital as well. Dedicated to sustainability not only in farming practices but also in relationships, J. Lohr Vineyards retains a full-time, year-round vineyard crew. The knowledge, energy, and experience

J. Lohr's twenty Monterey-based employees bring to the vineyards become flavor in the bottle. Turnover is the enemy of consistency and quality, and with very little change in top management in twenty-five years, J. Lohr's group represents one of the most dedicated and experienced teams in the industry.

Jerry's revolutionary stewardship of J. Lohr Vineyards and Wines continues to raise the bar for the entire industry. Constantly experimenting, he and master winemaker Jeff Meier are respected for their innovation and exacting standards. Referring to themselves as wine growers, not grape growers, these two leaders have been known to wait almost a decade after acquiring a property to begin planting grapes. Healthy, balanced soil is a key component to the advancement of flavor in wine. To achieve this, Jerry has created a vineyard development process that minimizes the use of commercial fertilizers by first planting nutrient-rich grain crops that are later harvested back into the soil. Though both labor intensive and expensive, this process fundamentally affects the quality and flavor of every grape.

Another defining J. Lohr process is their commitment to the use of night harvesting and field pressing. Night harvesting preserves the delicate freshness of the grapes, locks in flavor, and prevents premature fermentation. The press room is conveniently located in the vineyard, where the grapes are field pressed and crushed immediately after harvest while still cold, ensuring the extraction of the deepest fruit flavors.

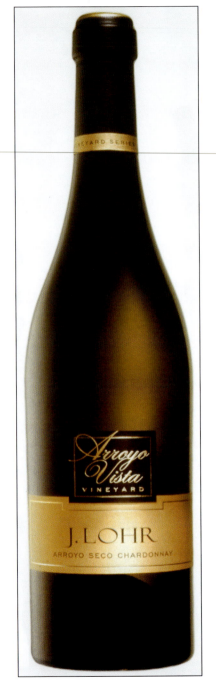

Though still run with the loving care of a boutique winery, J. Lohr has wisely invested in state-of-the art equipment and facilities. One of the few remaining substantial independents, J. Lohr produces only proprietor grown wines. Whether it's the J. Lohr Estates Riverstone Arroyo Seco Chardonnay, Estates Bay Mist Monterey White Riesling, Estates Wildflower Monterey Valdiguie or J. Lohr Arroyo Vista Vineyard Chardonnay, each wine is carefully nurtured to realize the full potential of its unique environment. This philosophy has paid off with J. Lohr wines consistently winning high praise and numerous awards for their notable excellence.

Over the years, Jerry has grown J. Lohr Vineyards and Wines with the same nurturing patience with which he's tended his beloved vineyards. While others have rushed to buy up blocks of land, feeding on Monterey's growing prestige, Jerry has been known to eye a piece of land for its ability to yield the most robust flavors, then to wait as long as a decade for it to become available. As a result, the original 280 acres of Arroyo Seco vineyards have slowly expanded to over 900 acres.

In the mid 1980s, J. Lohr took the next step and began planting reds. Taking a lesson from the French growing regions of Burgundy and Bordeaux, Jerry understood that great Chardonnay and Cabernet Sauvignon cannot grow side by side. Eager to explore new challenges, he began planting Cabernet Sauvignon, Merlot and other red varietals in San Luis Obispo's then little-known Paso Robles region.

Once more, Jerry found himself leading the way to a region that would quickly explode in popularity.

An elder statesman of the wine world, Jerry's passion for his work has earned him the respect of his peers and a dedicated following amongst those who appreciate ripe, rich   flavors in wines cultivated from one of the nation's most superb appellations — the Arroyo Seco region of Monterey County.

Ingenuity

Legacy of Clever Ingenuity . . .

. . . The Nielsen Brothers used their noggins. From the time they opened Nielsen Brothers Market in 1930, Harold and Walter applied their Danish family's heritage devising inventive strategies to meet the challenges of friendly rivalry with the dozen other grocery stores up and down Ocean Avenue in Carmel and become the stand-alone specialty food market and wine shop that they are today.

Early on their decision to offer home delivery, that included hand-selected produce and meats, brought them the acclaim they were looking for to outshine their local competition. The Carmel townspeople loved it. The Nielsen's genteel been-there-for-years staff knew each shopper's face and name, and assisted them with their purchases, helping them locate just the right item.

Harold and Walter expanded selections in all departments when they thought people might choose to shop there if they did. The Nielsens ensured that the customer received what they wanted, even if it meant getting it from another store to fill the order. As time went on, they became known, as the "You can count on them, they'll do it," Nielsen Brothers people.

The brothers used their wits and acute business sense to keep a good trade going so that they were not only able to survive, but to succeed during the depression and war years.

Along the way Walter's daughter Nancie had the good sense to marry the friendly college student who made Nielsen's' home deliveries and who loved the business as much as she did. After marrying the boss' daughter, Merv Sutton took the reins, applying his own sensibilities and eventually acquiring each brother's half of the business.

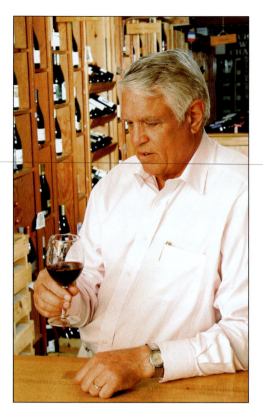

An ingenious exchange, with a little family help, started the young owner on his way. Merv's mother inherited a 440-acre ranch near Hollister. Walter always wanted to be a rancher. So the deal was struck: the ranch for half of the store. Thus, Walter became a rancher and Merv a half-store owner, later to fully own it when Harold retired.

As wine became a desired commodity, they opened up a downstairs room in the store just for their expanding collection of vintages. "The Wine Room" came alive in the lower level of the original market which opened in 1935, at Dolores and Eighth.

Merv invested in a real wine cellar with temperature controls and proper racks to lay bottles on their sides and keep them at their best. The expertise he developed in designing and organizing a wine cellar is still called upon today.

Merv saw that a market for winemaker dinners existed. He partnered with Carmel restaurants pairing wines to complement menus. They became so popular that the next dinner was sold out before the guests left the table at the previous one.

When the Wine Room became so busy that the clerks were continuously running up and down the stairs to tend to their customers on both floors, Merv decided that a wine consultant was very much needed. "The Wine Shop" was developed and together with the store was relocated to San Carlos and Seventh where it has thrived since 1980. Perhaps that longevity accounts for Nielsen Wine Shop's claim to have the first liquor license issued in Carmel since Prohibition was repealed. Since those early days, Nielsen's has had a professional to assist solely in the selection and tasting of wines. Nielsen's is now known as the home of fine domestic, imported and rare wines.

Tending the Wine Shop and Tasting Room for a dozen years now, Patrick Schrady is a true wine consultant with the depth of knowledge and necessary resources to lay hands on wines to pair with a special menu; to locate a wine or champagne the visitor had the last time they were in town or enjoyed at a friend's gathering; to order those extraordinary vintages from far and wide and to ship them to the far reaches as well; or just to suggest something different for tasting.

As the Nielsen legacy of innovation would have it, Christian, the third generation of the Nielsen Brothers, is applying himself to develop a new product line. Merv and Nancie's son is first, the produce manager, who can be seen putting his personal touch to the fresh produce displays inside and under the awning out front. Christian's tribute to his great uncles' adaptive marketing skills shows in his development of customized feast-for-the-eyes party trays, buffet arrangements, and fruit and gift baskets.

With the longevity, style and character wrought from Harold and Walter's legacy of devising ingenious business solutions, Nielsen Brothers Market and Wine Shop is a stand-alone Carmel institution, a.k.a. the Non-Supermarket. The brothers would be truly proud of Merv and Nancie Sutton, as they continue using their noggins to enhance the specialized care aspects of the store that Nancie's father and uncle created over seventy years ago.

–Karen Hunting

Love of Life

Passion for Wine, Love of Life . . .

. . . It is a whisper that echoes and calls telling of the welcoming ambiance and atmosphere that owners Patty and Bob Brower have enthused into their piece of heaven, Château Julien Wine Estate in Carmel Valley, California.

It was in the French countryside that Patty and Bob found and absorbed the comfortable, genteelness of the French winemakers. The cordial greeting extended to the Browers by the Chateau owners who met them personally, shared a glass of wine, conversation, and a tour with them, was exactly the ambiance they wanted for their own wine estate.

Once the Chateau's desired atmosphere was established in their minds, a site had to be chosen. Extensive travels throughout the state of California ultimately led the Browers to the acreage where the Chateau now resides in Carmel Valley.

First and foremost, Patty and Bob have fulfilled their dream by treating and including all those associated with Château Julien Wine Estate as family. For those working closely with them, the Browers extended an invitation to participate in planting and, ultimately, harvesting six acres of Sangiovese grapes. Each vine carried a label with the initials of the staff person who personally planted it that day. Celebrations at both the planting and the harvesting are Château Julien family affairs.

Over time each visitor joins their legion of friends and family in an intimate relationship with the French Chateau. Wine tasting at the grand mahogany table, guided tours through the vineyards, the Chai (a specialized wine aging house), and the Chateau itself, are conducted in a friendly, intimate atmosphere.

A special occasion, in which the Château Julien professionals (who tend the vineyards and the winemaking) like to include friends and guests, are the "crushings". The grapes are fresh off the vine, and brought to the huge stainless steel hopper where they are fed to a Demoisy crusher/stemmer. From that point the stems are removed from the grapes and the remaining "must" (juice and skins) is moved along for further processing. Red "must" is moved directly to

tanks for fermentation on the skins. White "must" is moved or pumped directly to the press and the juice is separated from the skins before fermentation. Onlookers are welcome to view, inhale the aromas, and photograph this first stage of winemaking that takes place right behind the Chateau itself.

And the invitations are readily accepted to come, enjoy, and participate in the private and community events held on the estate. This French-inspired hospitality extends to the nationally acclaimed Winemaker dinners, hosted in the wine cellars with a French market courtyard buffet. The country gardens and cobblestone pathways also set the tone for the annual open-air Wine & Art Festival, a community event.

The community, outside of the Chateau itself, also feels their generous support in wine donations for community efforts, in the public education of wines and to non-profit entities for fund-raising and awareness events.

Further evidence of Patty and Bob's desire to expand knowledge and appreciation of varietal wines is their Harvest Wine Seminar, held annually for a sold-out crowd. A family style dinner, pairing wines with the menu items, is hosted in the wine cellar near the gleaming stainless steel tanks.

If love of life, coupled with a passion for wine, can be brought from vision into reality, then the Brower's Château Julien Wine Estate is the graceful accomplishment of their French inspired dream of a wine estate that exudes welcome and warmth.

Patty and Bob Brower's lifelong desire to share their passionate love of life and wine, thus making wine an integral part of one's lifestyle, is clearly evident as friends, family and new-found friends are greeted in the Great Hall of the Chateau. A glass of wine, a friendly face, and the French-inspired cordiality continues from there.

–Karen Hunting

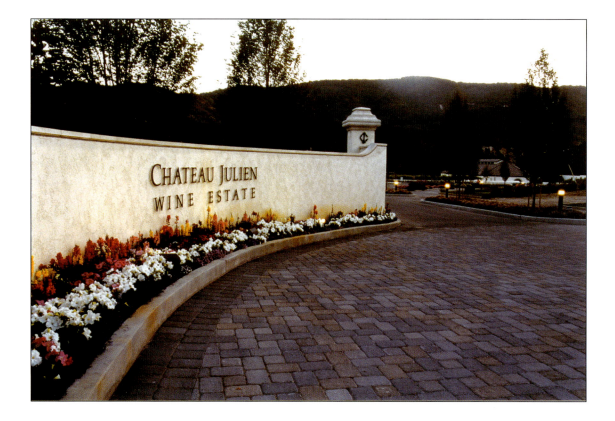

THE CYPRESS INN

Historic Hotel a Popular Gathering Place . . .

. . .The minute one crosses the threshold of the landmark Cypress Inn in Carmel-by-the-Sea, the first sound to escape is a luxurious sigh. The sense of coming home is as palpable as the scent of fresh flowers and the inviting warmth emanating from the lobby "living room" fireplace. It's futile to resist sinking into one of the comfy couches to bask in the ambiance or allowing the eyes to wander across the historic photographs and artworks that grace the walls. And, for those who join with co-owner Doris Day in a love of animals, the Inn is one of the area's best venues for enjoying the company of companions of the pet-persuasion.

The historic hotel, which opened in 1929 as *La Ribera*, was designed in the manner of Spain's Mediterranean buildings, making it at once distinctive and harmonious with the village's architecture. The 33-room inn is no get-lost-in-the-crowd accommodation as each guest, whether first-time or one of many return visitors, is treated like family. "Service is a hallmark of the Cypress Inn," says General Manager Hollace Thompson. "There's longevity with our staff so guests who visited two, five, even ten years ago are likely to see a familiar face." Locals often drop in to say hello, have tea or a glass of wine, giving guests the opportunity to mingle with local artists, celebrities and the cast of characters both two and four legged, who contribute to Carmel's charm.

In a visit to this Carmel-by-the-Sea treasure, it is not uncommon to be

joined by a powder puff of a Persian, a gangly Great Dane, a chic Shar-Pei or a slinky Siamese. The presence of pets is the distinctive stamp of dedicated animal-lover and -activist Doris Day. In 1988, this Hollywood darling and long-time Carmel resident joined highly respected hotelier Dennis LeVett as co-owner of the Cypress Inn and promptly laid out the "pets welcome" mat. To this day, that welcome goes well beyond an open door policy to feature dog-proof upholstered camel bag pillows in the living room, snacks, pet beds, litter boxes, leashes, a list of local restaurants that cater

to Fido and Morris, and a roster of at-the-ready pet sitters. And every year on Halloween, just as the fog dilutes the moonlight, a strange thing happens — pet lovers and their costumed canines and kitties from near and far descend upon the Inn for an impromptu indoor parade and costume contest.

"Our pet guests are primarily dogs and cats although we've had a few surprises over the years," says Hollace, "the llama of actress Kim Novak being a prime example. While the presence of beloved pets lends an air of informality and hominess to the Inn, the animals seem to sense the appropriate decorum and are polite, impeccably groomed and just as discriminating as their human companions."

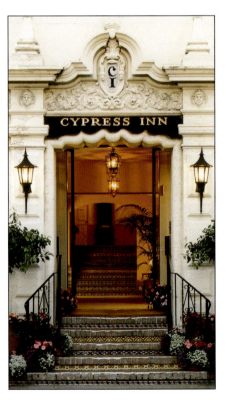

A typical evening at the Inn makes it easy to imagine that the setting is an elegant yet lively corner bistro in Paris or a bustling café along the Italian Riviera. While the Inn has long been a treasured venue where women introduce their granddaughters to afternoon tea, the cocktail-lounge-cum-wine-bar is quickly gaining a true following of its own.

With an impressive   selection of wines by the bottle and more than

20 by the glass, the Cypress Inn presents a true tasting opportunity. Showcasing the best of Monterey County's seven appellations as well as those from other regions of California and the world, the lounge equally pleases the palates of those with a taste for a dry white and those who love a lusty red. Thompson is constantly on the search for new attractions — the next likely to be enticing French and Spanish champagnes and sparkling wines.

Another of Thompson's innovations is evening tastings, some featuring scotches, and others ports. These events not only draw a sell-out crowd from the local scene, but also travelers have been known to plan a Carmel sojourn around them. Experts in the particular spirit are on hand to explain processes and pairings to ensure that a learning experience accompanies the sensory one.

The Cypress Inn is a delightful place to be, whether as an overnight guest, a day-visitor to the area or a local resident with a penchant for elegance and a homey, pet-friendly feel. A scrapbook in the living room recalls the experiences and comments of visitors, complete with photos of pets and "parents," who heartily agree.

—Melanie Belon Chatfield

ARROYO SECO VINEYARDS

Magical Wines from a Magical Place . . .

. . . There are wondrous little mini-regions throughout Monterey County. With the Gavilan Mountains on the eastern edge, the Santa Lucia range to the west and the incredible expanse of the Salinas Valley running straight down the middle, unlimited geographical and climatic conditions predominate. One of the most beautiful and important is the Arroyo Seco Appellation.

Located less than half way down the county near the little town of Greenfield, Arroyo Seco stretches west to the foot of the Santa Lucia Mountains. In the midst of vineyards as far as the eye can see, on a non-descript little road to nowhere in particular, a small, carefully manicured red house acts as the head-quarters for Arroyo Seco Vineyards.

A family owned grape-growing operation, Arroyo Seco Vineyards epitomizes the Monterey County wine scene. Agriculture has always been the number one reason for Monterey County's greatness. Arroyo Seco Vineyards continues that

tradition with its stunning array of vineyards located on various sites throughout the Arroyo Seco region.

The region, undeniable in its originality, is highlighted by an amazing gorge, cut by eons of the Arroyo Seco River's flow. This critical source of precious water refreshes all life around it, from the grapevine trim along the gorge's borders to wild animals like mountain lions and boar, to free running trout that gather in pools at various spots in the river during summer, unsuspectingly vulnerable to waiting anglers.

During the rainy season, the river grows angry and swells higher up the forty-foot tall walls of the gorge. Relentlessly stressed river banks and beds give way a

millimeter at a time as the raging river methodically etches its artistry into the Arroyo Seco landscape. And throughout it all, the grapevines peer over the gorge's edges, silent witnesses to nature's engineering marvel at work.

It always comes back to the grapevines. Throughout the year's various seasons, the vines carry on, calmly fulfilling their manifest destiny to produce delicious round berries of enchantment that will carry the memories of this wonderful setting to those wine drinkers fortunate enough to share in them.

Standing among the endless rows of trellised vines on a summer's afternoon while the newly budding grapes slowly absorb mother sun's nourishment, one is nearly overwhelmed by the serenity and calm. Magnificent vistas in every direction bathe the optic nerve in soothing images.

A feeling of humility at the majestic scope of the surroundings heightens the awareness as you begin to feel at home in the environment.

Cooling Pacific Ocean winds, a daily occurrence, temper the strong sunlight creating a fascinating full spectrum of temperature effect; at once warm and cool. Distant hills sit piled like giant suede pillows shaping shadows in mysterious canyons that beckon adventuresome spirits.

The flutter of vine canopies hypnotically serenades both visual and auditory sensors while countless chirps, warbles, screeches and whistles from the enormous bird population entertain and enliven the scene. The longer you stand there, the more aware you become of the cacophonous clamoring of activity all around—birds, insects, wind, earth, vines—nature's wonders at work.

Before long, you are intuitively understanding the entire cycle of life that farmers everywhere fully realize by tending their crops throughout the years. The splendor in the vineyard readily explains itself to your utterly receptive sensibilities and, though you may not understand the intricacies of winemaking, it becomes clearer how wine becomes an expression of this place, this land.

Over here, row after row of Chardonnay. Over there, Pinot Noir. Some Riesling to the left of you then look to another location and the columns of Cabernet Sauvignon march on. Step by regimented step they march, into rows of Merlot, then Shiraz, then Malbec, then Petit Verdot. They embody a veritable "clusters last stand" of gorgeous grape armies proudly holding against the onslaught of dusk.

It is no wonder so many wineries contract for the grapes of Arroyo Seco Vineyards. Savvy wine makers understand the many magical qualities transferred to grapes grown in magical places. The unique, completely individual characteristics of this special region comprise one facet of the jewel that is Monterey County. The sparkle of that jewel is evident in its wines.

—Ray Napolitano

Rising to the Challenge . . .

Challenge

. . . Centuries ago, before the first Europeans came to California, there was a sacred place, a place revered by the native Chumash people who lived there. To them, it was "anapamu," meaning "rising or ascending place." It was on the gently rolling foothills that overlook the fertile valley floor where the Chumash hunted and grew maize. Today, these hillsides and elevated plateaus are the ground where the grapes that are used to make some of the finest, most respected wines in the world are grown. This is Anapamu.

Anapamu wine grapes are grown at the Olson Ranch, west of Greenfield, in the Arroyo Seco AVA. The 330-acre vineyard is situated in the shadow of the Santa Lucias, a picturesque mountain range that shields the Salinas Valley from the Pacific and the bulk of its moisture and fog. The ranch is over 2,000 acres in total size, so there is room to grow.

The Greenfield area is dotted with century-old, steep-roofed wooden barns, survivors of one of the schemes of businessman David Jacks. Famous as the man who at one time owned the entire Monterey Peninsula, Jacks offered a plot of land to European—mostly Swiss—immigrants in exchange for raising dairy cattle on the land and selling the resulting products to him. The cows thrived on the land, which because of its high gravel content and poor moisture retention was unsuitable for growing traditional crops that require fertile soil and steady temperatures. But then again, premium wine grapes are not traditional crops.

In the foothills above the valley, the soil consists of a silty loam loaded with golf-ball-size and smaller granite gravel. This type of soil formation is called an alluvial fan, meaning that over the centuries, the mountains above have eroded and the resulting small stones have been washed to the land below by the actions of water and wind. The climate is considered cool; daytime temperatures during the growing season average around 80 degrees. Encroaching evening fog from the Monterey Bay chills the air, making this a perfect locale for growing-cool weather wine grapes such as Chardonnay, Sauvignon blanc, Pinot gris and Viognier.

These conditions allow the rows of vines to be planted closer together than they typically are on the valley floor. Anapamu grower Jon Winstead says that this type of shallow soil and planting style allow him to grow grapes that exhibit a nice balance between fruit and veggie (grassy, green) flavors.

Jon works very closely with winemaker Adam Richardson. Adam hails from Australia, where he gained experience with cool weather winemaking in the Yarra Valley, one of the most highly regarded growing regions Down Under. Throughout the growing season, Jon and Adam continuously test—and taste—the berries, making decisions on whether to trim leaves, thin out the fruit or adjust irrigation.

Irrigation is critical in the growing of wine grapes and several high-tech methods are utilized at the Olson Ranch. There are weather stations placed throughout the ranch that measure solar radiation, wind speed, temperature and humidity. These factors are computed to determine *evapotransporation*, a measurement of how much water the vines are using.

Another invaluable tool used by the grower is the scary-sounding *pressure bomb*. It's not as bad as it sounds. In this procedure, a leaf is inserted into a sealed chamber with the stem leading outside. The amount of water the leaf gives up when the chamber is pressurized is measured, giving another indication of how the plant is utilizing water. These techniques, among others, help Jon to fine-tune the irrigation schedule to stress the vines to just the right degree, producing the small, compact fruit exhibiting the desired structure of ripeness and acidity.

Anapamu grapes are harvested at night and are immediately transported to the winery in Healdsburg to keep them cool. Heat would upset that delicate sugar/acid balance that the grower has so carefully nurtured over the summer. Then Adam goes to work. "We want to produce a wine that showcases the rich, deep, ripe fruit flavors of the grapes that we grow in Monterey County," he says.

The goal, Adam says, is to produce a predominant richness in the wine that is instantly recognizable as Anapamu. Bright, high-toned flavors predominate in these wines. They pair perfectly with many types of cuisine, complimenting foods while not being overbearing or overwhelming. Anapamu is not a huge enterprise by wine industry standards. Just 40,000-50,000 cases are produced a year, allowing the makers to concentrate on getting the wine just right. And the world at large approves. In only the five short years of its existence, the Chardonnay, Pinot Noir and Riesling that Anapamu produces in Monterey County have gone head to head with wines from all over the world and have emerged victorious, winning top awards in Jerry Mead's New World International Wine Competition, The San Francisco Chronicle Wine Competition, The California State Fair Wine Competition, and the Taster's Guild Wine Competition among others. Anapamu is also known for an award-winning Syrah that is grown in the warmer climate of Paso Robles, south of Monterey County.

The language of the Chumash people has provided a word that perfectly describes the growing region, and, in a sense the future of Anapamu. And Anapamu is producing wines that do justice to that heritage. A rising star in the wine galaxy, Anapamu is definitely ascending to the heights of greatness.

—Michael Chatfield

Wine Tasting Map

PINNACLES

CHALONE **20**

Soledad

ROBERT MONDAVI
PRIVATE SELECTION

THE MONTEREY
VINEYARD

Chualar

Gonzales

13 **14** **15**

RIVER ROAD
VINEYARDS

BLACKSTONE
WINERY

SAN SABA

HAHN
ESTATES/
SMITH
& HOOK

CLONINGER
PAVONA WINES

MORGAN

JOYCE WINERY/
CHATEAU CHRISTINA

Salinas

A TASTE OF
MONTEREY

12

Abbott

Spreckles

River Road

HELLER ESTATE

TALBOTT

BERNARDUS

PARSONAGE
VILLAGE VINEYARD

5 **6** **7**

DE TIERRA
VINEYARDS

VENTANA
VINEYARDS/
MEADOR
ESTATE

BAYWOOD
CELLARS

2

Monterey

A TASTE OF
MONTEREY

1

Pebble Beach

Carmel

68 **218**

3

Del Monte

Munras

CHATEAU
JULIEN

4

JOULLIAN

Carmel Valley
Village

CHATEAU SINNET

SAN SABA

8 **9** **10**

GALANTE

11

Big Sur

Reservation Road

Carmel Valley Road

Laureles Grade

Monterey-Salinas Hwy

Cachagua Road

Tassajara Road

San Francisco

Monterey County

Los Angeles

Monterey

CONTRIBUTOR CONTACT INFORMATION

A Taste of Monterey Wine Visitors' Center, Monterey and Salinas

Oldtown Salinas, 127 Main Street
Salinas, CA 93901
831.751.1980
www.tastemonterey.com
Tasting: M-Sat 11am-5pm

Cannery Row, 700 Cannery Row, (Upstairs)
Monterey, CA 93940
831.646.5446/831.375.0835 fax
www.tastemonterey.com
Tasting: Daily 11am-6pm

Our visitors' centers showcase wines from over 40 Monterey County wineries. Located one block from the world-renowned Monterey Bay Aquarium, the Cannery Row wine center is graced with a panoramic view of the entire bay. Enjoy tasting while viewing entertaining and educational exhibits. Expert wine consultants will gladly answer a wide array of questions regarding Monterey County's wineries, wine production and history. The Oldtown Salinas center is located just steps away from the National Steinbeck Center.

Anapamu Cellars
35422 Paraiso Springs Road
Soledad, CA 93960
5585 Creston Road
Paso Robles, CA 93446
Tasting: A Taste of Monterey

Anapamu-pronounced "AH-NUH-PAH-MU"-means "rising place" in the Native American Chumash language-and signifies the rising hills surrounding our vineyards. Our Olson Ranch, named after pioneering cattle rancher Otto Olson, has approximately 335 acres under vine-primarily Chardonnay and Pinot Noir-located in the heart of the Santa Lucia Highlands appellation.

Arroyo Seco Vineyards
Greenfield, CA
Contact: Sandy Flanders
800.778.0424
No Tasting Room

Arroyo Seco Vineyards grows grapes and crafts fine wines for some of California's most celebrated wineries. They produce Chardonnay and Pinot Noir under their own label, Arroyo del Sol, *arroyo* of the sun, as well as wines under the Stel Creek and Muirwood brands. Owned by the Zaninovich family, pioneers in Monterey County wine grape growing, their vineyards in the Arroyo Seco Appellation include prime viticultural property with the Arroyo Seco River carving a majestic gorge through it.

Blackstone Winery

800 South Alta Street
Gonzales, CA 93926
831.675.5341
831.675.8923 fax
www.blackstonewinery.com
Tasting: 11am-4pm daily;
Picnic Area; Special Events

Visit the Blackstone Winery to taste our delicious wines, experience our rotating art exhibit and picnic on our lovely grounds. Blackstone Winery is planted in the Monterey appellation with Chardonnay, Merlot, Pinot Noir, Cabernet Sauvignon and Sauvignon Blanc.

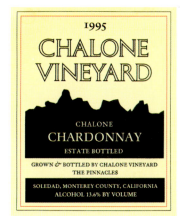

Chalone Vineyard

P.O. Box 518, Soledad, CA 93960
831.678.1717
831.678.2742 fax
www.chalonevineyard.com

A pioneer in the California wine industry, Chalone Vineyard began in 1919 in an area so distinctive, it was granted its own American Viticulture Area. This remote vineyard is perched high in the Gavilan Mountain Range on limestone-rich soil. This spare, well-drained land, with its limited rainfall and low crop levels produces wines with a full bouquet and hedonistic flavor unique to this vineyard. We specialize in Chardonnay, Pinot Noir, Pinot Blanc, Chenin Blanc and Syrah.

Château Julien Wine Estate

8940 Carmel Valley Road
Carmel, CA 93923
831.624.2600
831.624.6138 fax
www.chateaujulien.com
Tasting: 8am-5pm Mon-Fri,
11am-5pm weekends
Tours:
Mon-Fri, 10:30am & 2:30pm;
Weekends 12:30pm & 2:30pm
Picnic Area; Special Events

Château Julien Wine Estate is located on 16 acres in the majestic Carmel Valley, a short 5-minute drive from Carmel. Guests are welcome daily for wine tasting and tours of Château Julien. Enjoy a picnic in the beautiful garden cobblestone courtyard. Château Julien Wine Estate's vineyards are located in the Monterey appellation planted with Cabernet Sauvignon, Chardonnay, Merlot, Pinot Grigio, Sangiovese, Sauvignon Blanc, Syrah and Zinfandel.

Cypress Inn

Lincoln & 7th, P.O. Box Y
Carmel, CA 93923
831.620.1234
831.626.1575 fax
800.443.7443
www.cypress-inn.com

Cypress Inn, located in the heart of Carmel-by-the-Sea, is an important part of the   history and tradition of this beautiful area. Known for its classic interior, stately exterior and recognized by its Moorish Mediterranean facade, in brilliant white, with Spanish tiled roof. This beautiful inn has been restored to the beauty and grace, which has characterized it for the past seven decades. Pets are also welcome.

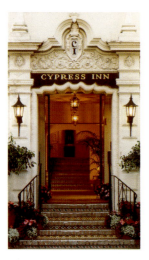

Estancia

1775 Metz Road
Soledad, CA 93960
831.678.0214
831.678.9368 fax
www.estanciaestates.com
Tasting: A Taste of Monterey

Estancia's President, Agustin Francisco Huneeus, believes that great wines are a reflection of their terroir. As a result, every vintage of Estancia Chardonnay and Pinot Noir, is a stylistic expression of our Pinnacles Vineyard. Estancia's vineyards are planted in the Monterey and Santa Lucia Highlands appellations to Chardonnay and Pinot Noir, as well as fifty acres of experimental vineyards.

Fandango Restaurant

223 17th Street
Pacific Grove, CA 93921
831.372.3456
831.372.2673 fax
www.fandangorestaurant.com
Open every day. Lunch, Dinner and Sunday Brunch
Full Bar
Reservations encouraged
Private Parties for 8-50 guests

In the warmth of a Mediterranean setting, experience the spirited, flavorful foods of European Country-Style Cuisine...fresh seafood, steaks, rack of lamb, pastas, paellas, the valley's best vegetables, and of course, wine. Pierre and Marietta Bain have created an exceptional dining atmosphere that is both casual and elegant. Food, Fun, Fandango.... an experience you'll never forget!

Hames Valley Vineyards

P.O. Box 450
Bradley, CA 93426
805.472.4963

Hames Valley Vineyards is located in a small coastal valley in rural Monterey County just north of Paso Robles. The Denney family began to grow their winegrape vineyards in Hames Valley in 1988. They produce premium Cabernet, Merlot, and Syrah wine grapes. They pursue their living with the vineyards, raising purebred Gelbvieh cattle, and breeding and showing their huge, beautiful Percheron draft horses.

Growing throughout the property are Cabernet Sauvignon, Merlot, Cabernet Franc and Syrah. Blocks of Zinfandel, Petite Verdot, Sauvignon Blanc and Viognier are also here.

J. Lohr Winery

1000 Lenzen Avenue
San Jose, CA 95126
408.288.5057
www.jlohr.com
Tasting: 10am-5pm daily

6169 Airport Blvd.
Paso Robles, CA 93446
805.239.8900
Picnic Area in Paso Robles only,
Special Events in San Jose and
Paso Robles.

Celebrating more than 25 years of estate produced wines of extraordinary quality, J. Lohr Winery is proud of its Riverstone Chardonnay, Wildflower Valdiguié, Bay Mist White Riesling and its newest single vineyard Chardonnay "Arroyo Vista". J. Lohr's Monterey County vineyards are located in the Arroyo Seco appellation and consist of over 900 acres of Chardonnay, Pinot Blanc, Valdiguié and White Riesling.

Jekel Vineyards

40155 Walnut Avenue
Greenfield, CA 93927
831.674.5525
831.674.3769 fax
1-800.625.2610
www.usawines.com/jekel
Tasting: 11am-4pm daily
Picnic Area; Special Events

Founded by Bill Jekel, vineyard planting began in 1972 with the first vintage release in 1978. The Gravelstone Vineyard and Sanctuary Estate are the cornerstones of Jekel's vineyard properties. Encounter the true flavors of our wines, from Chardonnay to Petit Verdot and you will soon understand Jekel's commitment to excellence in fulfilling the promise of Monterey. Jekel Vineyards is located in the Arroyo Seco appellation, planted with Cabernet Franc, Cabernet Sauvignon, Chardonnay Malbec, Merlot, Petit Verdot, Pinot Noir and Riesling.

Mer Soleil Vineyard

P.O. Box 35, Rutherford, CA 94573
831.675.7017
mersoleilwinery@aol.com
Tasting: A Taste of Monterey

Located in the Santa Lucia Highlands appellation of Monterey County, Mer Soleil winery produces a lush tropical style of Chardonnay. Both vineyard and winery are the work of father and son team, Chuck and Charlie Wagner. Additional varieties grown on the vineyard include Marsanne, Pinot Blanc, Pinot Gris and Viognier.

Monterey County Vintners and Growers Association

P.O. Box 1783
Monterey, CA 93942-1793
831.375.9400
831.375.1116 fax
www.montereywines.org
email: info@montereywines.org

Founded in 1974, MCVGA is a non-profit organization established to promote Monterey County as a world-class grape growing and wine producing area. MCVGA is comprised of over 65 growers and vintners who nurture the grapes and craft the wines of the magnificent region. Monterey County boasts over 45,000 acres planted in varietal wine grapes.

Nielsen Brothers Market

San Carlos & 7th, NE Corner
P.O. Box H
Carmel by-the-Sea, CA 93921
831.624.6441 (grocery)
831.624.WINE (wine)
831.624.3170 Fax
email: market@nielsenbros.com

"The best wines from the great wine producing countries all over the world." Wine tasting daily, 8am-8 pm. Visit our meat counter and select from the finest aged black angus beef, fresh fish, cheese, and deli selections. We also carry fresh produce, gourmet foods and liquors from around the world. Gift baskets and cheese trays made to order and home delivery. Not your typical market!

Passionfish Restaurant

701 Lighthouse Ave.
Pacific Grove, CA 93950
831.655.3311

Passionfish Restaurant offers a uniquely Californian dining experience, with serious food and wine in a fun and casual atmosphere. The ever changing menu offers the freshest seafood, prime steaks, slow cooked meats, farm fresh greens, and delectable house-made desserts complemented with a Wine Spectator award winning wine list, priced well below what you might expect. Passionfish is open for dinner 6 nights a week from 5pm, and closed on Tuesdays. Banquets and private parties are welcome.

The Sardine Factory Restaurant

701 Wave Street
Monterey, CA 93940
831.373.3775
www.sardinefactory.com

For over 33 years, Monterey's premier seafood restaurant, also serving prime meats and innovative cuisine. The wine list has been a Wine Spectator Grand Award recipient since the award's inception, and the gracious service and elegant ambiance are the perfect complement to a memorable fine dining experience.

Ventana Vineyards/Meador Estate

2999 Monterey-Salinas Hwy # 10
Monterey, CA 93940
831.372.7415
831.655.1855 fax
www.ventanawines.com
www.meadorestate.com
Tasting: 11am-5pm daily (Oct-May),
11am-6pm (June-Sept)
Picnic Area; Special Events

Ventana Vineyards and Meador Estate's recipe of innovation, research and artistic vision has consistently produced a tasteful combination for over 20 years. Sample our award-winning wines at our tasting room, just 5 minutes from downtown Monterey in the Old Stone House. The vineyards are planted in the Arroyo Seco appellation.

119

PHOTOGRAPHY CREDITS

Special thanks to the many local and regional photographers that contributed to this book, including: Wayne Holden, Wayne Capili, Margaretha Maryk, Batista Moon, Patrick Tregenza

AUTHORS CREDITS

Melanie and Michael Chatfield are freelance writers who live and work in Monterey, California. Karen Hunting owns and operates Artful Marketing Solutions in Carmel, California. Ray Napolitano works in the wine industry and writes for various publications.

ORDERING INFORMATION

For more information about *WineStyle Monterey County* or to order another copy, please visit **www.baypublishing.com** or call **(831) 373-8949**, Monday through Friday. You may also submit your requests by mail addressed to: Bay Publishing Company

395 Del Monte Center, #103

Monterey, CA 93940

Fax (831) 373-0290